Are We There Yet?
All About the Planet Uranus!
Space for Kids
Children's Aeronautics & Space Book

BABY PROFESSOR

EDUCATION KIDS

Uranus is the seventh planet from the Sun.

Uranus boasts a majestic blue/green haze because of methane gas.

Uranus is rolling like a barrel instead of spinning like the Earth and other planets.

Uranus was the first planet discovered using a telescope.

It takes 84
Earth years
for Uranus
to go around
the sun.

Its atmosphere is mostly hydrogen and methane.

Uranus cannot be seen by the naked eye, but it can be seen using a telescope.

In 1787,
Uranus was
first seen
by William
Herschel.

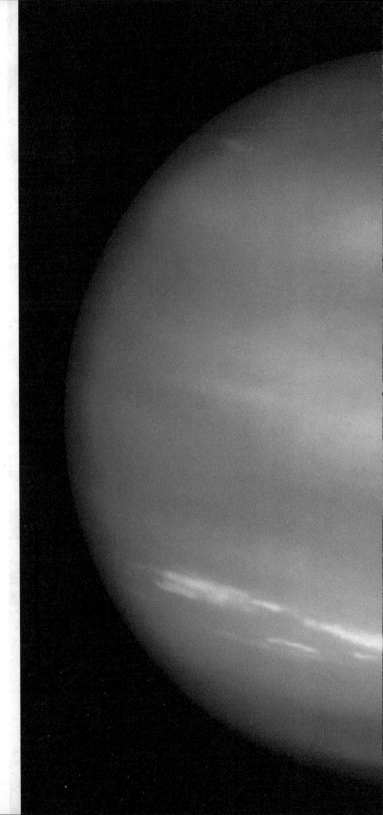

Herschel also discovered 2 of Uranus' moons.

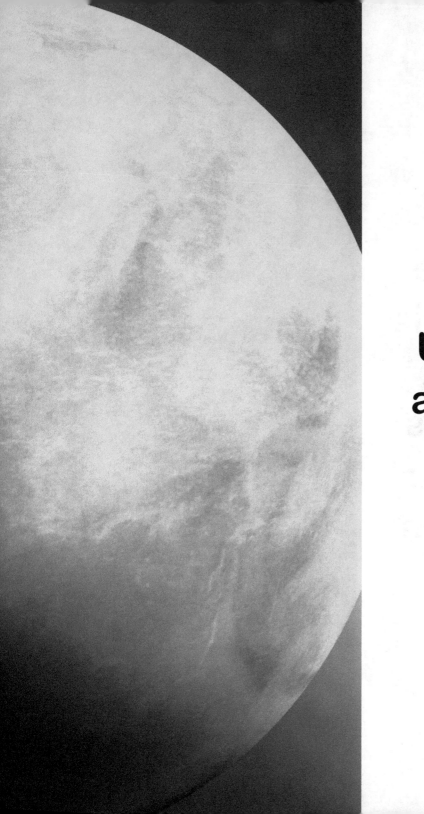

Uranus has
a total of 27
moons.

Most of the center of this planet is a frozen mass of ammonia and methane.

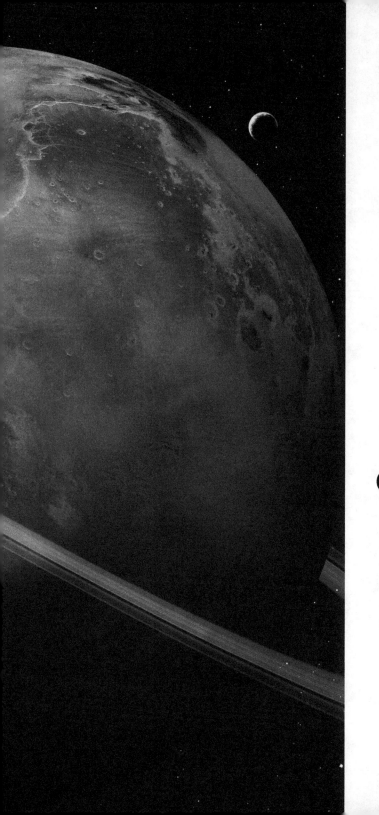

It takes 17.9 hours for Uranus to turn on its own axis.

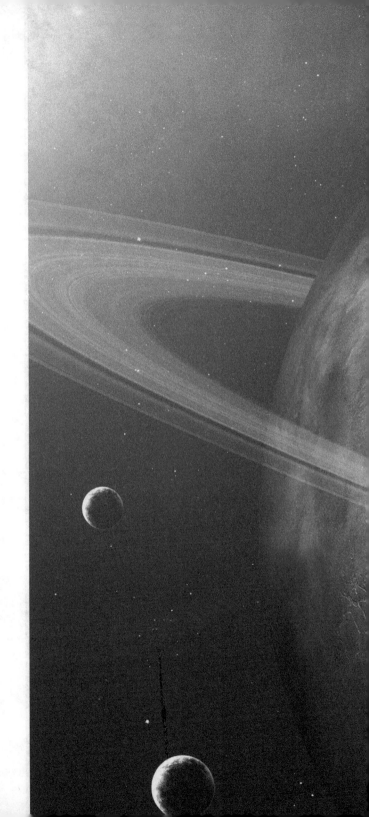

Uranus was named after the ancient Greek God of the heavens.

Uranus is
the smallest
of the four
giant planets.

Uranus is 1,782 million miles away from the sun.

The planet
has eleven
very faint
rings.

Scientists have not yet discovered exactly what causes those rings or what they are made of.

Uranus' temperature is almost always the same.

Research and learn more about the planet URANUS! Have fun!

Visit

BABY PROFESSOR
EDUCATION KIDS

www.BabyProfessorBooks.com

to download Free Baby Professor eBooks
and view our catalog of new and exciting
Children's Books

9 781683 269267